The Wedding Guidebook

How to save thousands of dollars and still have the wedding of your dreams!

D.P. Scott

DEDICATION

To Alexandra and Tyson

CONTENTS

THE WEDDING GUIDEBOOK

Planning a wedding can be stressful and time consuming. It is an emotional event, one you may have dreamt about your whole life, and a time when you can be talked into spending much more money than was originally budgeted. Because there are so many things to consider when planning the big day, if you are not organized with set budgets for every item, you can wind up in debt. Today, a traditional wedding with around one hundred guests can cost $30,000 or more. Many couples start off their lives together with wedding debt taking years to pay off the loan, and parents have been known to take out a second mortgage on their house to pay for a child's wedding. But what if there was a way to cut the average cost of a wedding by more than a third. The old saying: "You can't have your cake and eat it too," is wrong, you can!

We put on our daughter's wedding, a formal 110 guest affair, for under $10,000. There was a string quartet playing music for the ceremony, a professional photographer taking pictures, a formal sit down dinner reception and live entertainment. It involved a lot of planning, organizing, and delegating, which involved relatives, friends, and neighbours; however the wedding and reception went off without a hitch.

When our daughter became engaged in September and told us they planned to wed the following July, I immediately became concerned. Because I had done event planning as part of my job, I knew it would be difficult to find a venue for the wedding, not just because we only had ten months, but because July was in the middle of wedding season. Sure enough, every place I called was already booked. With no venue, and my daughter's heart set on the date, it suddenly occurred to me that we could have the wedding in our own backyard. This decision ended up being a blessing. Not only could we have the event the exact day she wanted, but our daughter was to be married at the house where she grew up. She and her fiancé loved the idea. Now, I want you to understand that we live on an average street, in an average house. Our yard is slightly larger than normal with an oversized cherry tree, but our flower beds were nothing to write home about. However, when the day of the wedding arrived, the yard had been transformed into a Garden of Eden--at least pretty close to one. Friends and neighbours couldn't believe what we had accomplished. And the funny thing was that the process had been easy!

In this guidebook, I have included instructions on everything you need to consider (also, I have included the average cost). I talk about decisions you need to make, how you need to prepare for the big day, and give suggestions and tips on how you can save a lot of money. From traditions, wedding invitations, all the way to how to plan and execute a killer reception, I offer cost saving ideas. Whether you have decided to have your wedding in a church or outdoors in a city park, university or botanical garden, winery, golf course, beside a beautiful waterway, or have a destination wedding-- there are ways to save money. Often these are things the wedding professionals won't tell you. In this guidebook you will also find food suggestions with simple, elegant and tested recipes (appetizers, salads, and desserts), which can be prepared in advance, including a wedding cake recipe and other cake options. If you are willing to roll up your sleeves and do some of the ground work, you can have a beautiful, memorable day for a fraction of the cost of a totally catered affair.

Now remember, you don't have to do everything yourself. The cost of the event totally depends on how much money you want or don't want to spend on your big day. The most expensive parts of a wedding event are the food and liquor (a catered lunch or dinner will cost $75-$200 and up, per guest), photographer ($1000-$4000), and venue and entertainment ($3000-$10,000). If you hire a wedding planner, add another $3000-$5000 to the tally. The other big ticket items are the wedding gown, ($300 and up), the wedding cake, which if professionally made will cost at least $900 or more, and the flowers, which include pots of flowers, bouquets, and boutonnieres--if purchased from a florist these can run up to 8-10% of the total wedding budget.

We were able to cut costs in every one of the above expenses, and in several ways, which I explain in detail below. I became the wedding planner, organizing and running the event up until the wedding day. For the wedding day, I hired a woman to run the kitchen and six young women to serve and clean up. I pre-made some of the food, and the wedding cake, and we used our own backyard, thus avoiding venue charges. You can have the wedding of your dreams at a reasonable cost if you are willing to do some of the work. And by just becoming your own wedding planner, you will save thousands of dollars. Whether it is the bride, the bride's mother, or a friend taking the lead on the wedding, it has to be someone who is organized and responsible. You will need to have a planning board and planning book where all the information, lists, key names, phone numbers, and receipts are kept and a check list, especially if you want to do the whole event yourself.

The Wedding Date

Obviously, the first thing to consider with an outdoor wedding and reception is the weather. Consult the Farmer's Almanac and look back at previous years to see if it rained on the day you have selected. Think about borrowing or renting tent awnings in case it is very hot or does shower (the cost to rent is $110 each). I was surprised to find out how many of our friends had awnings, so ask around. We were able to borrow six 10x10 open sided awnings for the wedding day.

Of course, if you are having a church wedding and indoor reception weather isn't as much of an issue.

Invitations

You have several options for invitations. Formal invitations made by a printing company are lovely, but expensive, even if you order them from the internet. Consider making them yourself. It is easy to do. Buy blank cards from the internet or from the wedding section at a craft store (Tip: if you purchase from a craft store, look for discount coupons on the internet. Sometimes you can print off a coupon or download an App for 40% off the retail value). Go to a wedding invitation site for ideas on how to word the invitation. A recent trend is to request the attendance response by email. This saves on the cost of stamps, as you are expected to pay for the stamp on the response card. If you choose to go the email response route, you can then use the response card (usually comes in the package when you purchase invitations) as a gift thank you card. The other option is to send the wedding invitation by email, although it is considered more elegant to receive an invitation by mail. Wedding invitations should be sent out 2-4 months in advance of the wedding. For a destination wedding, 8 months is suggested so that guests will have time to make travel plans.

There are many free or low-cost interactive wedding websites, which have a photo page, space to post information about the wedding couple, and a place that people can RSVP to your wedding. My daughter used one of these sites to create a personal page for her big day. By using a wedding tool site, you will be able to have all of your responses in one area, and have an accurate tally of the number of guests attending. You can also use this site to post your gift registry, post directions to the ceremony and reception, and list hotels where you have pre-arranged special rates for overnight guests. (Tip: most hotels will block 10 or more rooms at a special discounted rate for weddings. If your wedding is during the tourist season, and you expect many out-of-town guests, book a hotel close to the venue as soon as possible). Be aware that not everyone has access to a computer. If you plan to receive your RSVPs by email or through a wedding website, make sure to also add a phone number.

The Venue

Indoor wedding

If you are planning a church wedding, the cost of using the church will be $350-$3,500, which includes the fees for the use of the church, organist and cantor, wedding director, and cleanup. A monetary gift to the minister or priest is also expected ($150-$300). To save money, consider using the church basement for the reception, as sometimes there will be no other charge or rental fee. Usually there are tables, chairs and a kitchen. However, be aware that if you do use the church basement for the reception, liquor and dancing may not be allowed.

Another cost saving idea for an indoor reception is to use the clubhouse of a condominium development. Residents living in the development can rent the room for a reasonable rate ($50-$500). And often the clubhouse already has tables and chairs available as well as a kitchen. Hotel meeting or ballrooms are another option, but be prepared to possibly have to pay a rental fee ($150-$1500) and also be forced to use the catering services of the hotel. (The rental fee depends on the number of guests you guarantee to attend, which means you have to pay for their dinner whether or not they come to the wedding) This is the most expensive way to go. Local neighbourhood halls with tables and chairs that are available for rent ($300-$1,000) will often have kitchens for food preparation (see the food section for ideas on what to serve). If you use a hall or clubhouse, you will also be responsible for the decorating and cleanup. Some universities are now offering meeting and banquet halls for wedding ceremonies and receptions. University catering services are also offered at some sites at more reasonable rates than restaurants.

Outdoor wedding

For an outdoor wedding, a quick sketch of the outdoor space is necessary. Plan where the ceremony will take place. It could be under a tree, a pergola, an arbor or a simple archway made out of lattice. Mark out where the guests will sit and allow an aisle for the bride to walk down. You will need approximately 24 x 52 feet of space for 110 chairs, which gives you a 4 foot aisle, and a 6 foot area for the wedding party at the front. Decide on the best bridal route to the place you have selected for the ceremony.

If the ceremony is at a city or regional park, university or botanical garden, winery, or golf course, expect to pay a rental fee for the use of the grounds ($100-$500). You will also be responsible for renting the chairs from a rental company, transporting them, and removing them, and any litter following the nuptials. A winery or golf course will expect you to have your reception at the restaurant or clubhouse. If the ceremony is during golf season, the reception will most likely be delegated to a side banquet room.

If you are considering a winery or golf course for the event, you will need to book the venue 12 to 24 months in advance, especially if the wedding date falls on a Saturday. To reduce the cost, consider having a morning wedding with a stand up reception. You can serve trays of appetizers, and desserts, and instead of an open bar or wine and beer only, serve punch. ($50 and up, per guest) A sit down brunch or luncheon is another option, ($70 and up, per guest). Some winery and golf course venues require a minimum amount of money to be spent on the event. If all the Saturdays are booked, consider having the wedding Friday evening or Sunday morning. If most of your guests are local, a mid-week wedding could also be a practical option.

By using a backyard as the venue, you will not only eliminate rental fees for the outdoor space, you will have more time to get the space ready. If you plan an outdoor sit down lunch or dinner, you will need another 24 x 52 feet, (48 x 104 feet total) to seat 110 people. Round tables (60 inch diameter) can seat up to 10 people (a bit tight), and 9 guests very comfortably. Rectangular tables: 6 foot seats 8 people, 8 foot seats up to 10 people. Following the ceremony, have assigned people set up the tables, using the chairs from the ceremony for the reception. The rental charge for tables are approximately $12-$15 each, chairs are $2-$4.25 each. (See rental section below for prices and other items you will need such as tablecloths, dishes, etc)

Often, you can rent a beautiful space at a city or regional park for the ceremony. If the park has a picnic area, this could be a potential place for an informal type of reception. (See food suggestions and recipes below). Usually you will only be allowed to have the ceremony in a botanical or university garden.

Priests and some ministers will only officiate a church

wedding. You may have to hire a justice of the peace for an outdoor wedding (cost $100-$400).

Destination Weddings

The thought of a destination wedding sounds exciting and although it might be the right choice for you, be aware that the prices advertised on the internet are for the very basic of services. (Average cost, not including travel or accommodation is $5,000-$30,000 and up). The cost may seem within your means, but be aware this is because you usually have fewer guests attending. For this type of wedding you will likely need to hire a wedding planner at the location and have him or her organize the whole event, including accommodation for the guests. To lower the cost, consider having the wedding during the destination's low season. To offset the cost of guest travel, wedding gifts are often waived.

The advantage of a destination wedding is the built-in honeymoon. However, take note that many of the guests will stay on following the wedding, making the honeymoon less private. Another important note is that a marriage ceremony in some countries is not recognized back home. You may be required to have a civil ceremony upon return. Some countries also have different requirements to obtain a marriage license, such as health tests, or residence in that country for x number of days prior to the ceremony.

Adventure Weddings

For thrill seekers with money to burn, consider an adventure wedding. You can choose from a bungee jumping, underwater (special mask with mouth piece to say vows), or sky-diving ceremony, to having it in an aquarium, zoo, cave, on a rollercoaster at an amusement park, or at one of Disneyland's many venues such as Cinderella's castle. This type of wedding may not be for the budget conscious couple, but if it is what you want, consider inviting fewer guests to save on the reception costs of food and drink.

Wedding Attire

The cost of a wedding gown can exceed $10,000, with the average bridal store gown ranging from $300-$2,000. Most brides have an idea of what they want, but are unprepared for the cost. If you find a gown that is over-the-top expensive, but is exactly what you want, take a picture (bridal stores don't want you to do this) and consider having it made. You can also look in bridal magazines for the style you want and take the picture to a tailor. A good tailor will charge about $800 to make a gown. One idea is to consider a vintage wedding gown, borrowed from a mother, aunt, grandmother or friend, and have it altered to fit. Another option is to watch for bridal gown sales or consider ordering an overly fancy bridesmaid's dress in white.

If the wedding is outdoors make sure the bride and bridesmaids have shoes without stiletto heels, as you don't want the bridal party sinking down into the grass with every step.

A wedding veil is expensive to buy, but easy to make. For a simple double layered veil, measure from the top of the head to the desired veil length. Double this measurement and add 10 inches. Purchase tulle fabric (traditionally used for veils and very reasonable to buy) in the desired color to match your dress. Make sure the tulle is at least 60 inches wide. Fabric has a selvage edge (the finished or lengthwise edges) and a raw edge (the cut edges at either end of the fabric). To make a finished looking half circle for the bottom of the veil, you need to fold your fabric (remember it is a double layered veil), first in half so the cut edges line up (don't worry if they aren't exact, you will fix that. This is the bottom of the veil. The folded end is the top of the veil). Now fold the fabric lengthwise so that the selvage edges line up (this is more important to line up as these are the sides of the veil). You should now have four thicknesses of tulle. Start cutting the raw edge of the fabric on the folded side and cut a half circle ending up at the selvage edge side. When you open the veil back up, you should have an even and neat half circle on the bottom of the veil. Using a needle and invisible thread, gather the top folded edge and sew onto a clear colored hair comb. Pearls, rhinestones and/or ribbon roses (available at craft or fabric stores) can be sewn onto the gathered edge to make a headpiece. Pearls and rhinestones can also be used to adorn the veil by randomly sewing them onto the top layer.

The bridesmaids are responsible to pay for their own dresses. If time permits, check out the after-Christmas sales for fancy holiday dresses.

Although there is no set rule about attire for the groom and groomsmen, it gives a more elegant ambiance to a wedding ceremony when the men in the wedding party are formally dressed. The groom and groomsmen can rent tuxedos ($100-$200 for the day), or to economize, the groom can wear a suit or tuxedo and the groomsmen can wear black pants with matching vests. Another option is to forego the vests for white shirts, matching ties, and suspenders. The groomsmen are responsible to pay for their own attire.

Flowers

Flowers make a wedding. You will need potted flowers for the ceremony and of course, bouquets, and boutonnieres. Consider flowers that will be in full bloom on the big day. For a church ceremony, you can use vases of cut flowers and adorn the aisle pews with one cut or artificial flower tied with a ribbon bow. If the wedding is to be held in your backyard, pick colors to compliment the wedding theme and plant them in the garden beds and in large ornamental pots. Make sure to consult with your garden center about blooming times. We even had hanging baskets in the trees. Instead of purchasing large pots of flowers, which can be expensive, pre-order hanging baskets from a garden center ($30.00-$40.00 each), cut off the metal hanging hooks, and plop the whole hanging basket, plastic container and all, into correctly sized decorative pots. (I painted cheaply purchased clay pots black to make them look more elegant). Using a hanging basket for this purpose is lovely because it is usually overstuffed with plants and includes trailing flowers.

For the wedding bouquets and boutonnieres, consider making them yourself. Ordering flowers from the florist is very expensive. On the morning of the rehearsal (usually the rehearsal is the day before the wedding), pick up bouquets of flowers (one or two for the bride and one for each of the bridesmaids) from a large box store (approximately $14-$24), split up the bouquets and place them in buckets of water. Also from a dollar store, pick up florist wire, tape, and pearl ended hat pins (for the boutonnieres). Buy wide ribbon from a craft store to compliment or match the wedding colors. Before or after the rehearsal lunch or dinner have the bride and each one of the bridesmaids make their own bouquet. The mother of the flower girl can make hers, and anyone including the groom can make the boutonnieres. The bride should be allowed to select her flowers first. (For tips on how to make bouquets, and boutonnieres look at videos on the internet) It is very easy and fun, and only takes about twenty minutes. Place the finished bouquets in mason jars with enough water to cover the stems. Boutonnieres should be placed in the fridge. Any leftover flowers can be used to decorate the house.

Photographer

Photographers are expensive and usually charge depending on the number of hours they are at the wedding. If they take pictures of the bride getting ready and stay until the end of the reception, expect to pay a hefty price. You can save thousands of dollars by having the photographer only take pictures during the ceremony and pictures of the wedding party following the nuptials. Ask two or three friends to take pictures of the reception. Use a photographer recommended by family or friends, and check out their work before you hire them. Discuss package options. With the convenience of digital photography, some photographers may provide pictures as well as a disc where you can print off more of your favorite pictures. If you would like a video of the event, consider asking a friend. A videographer can charge from $1500-$3000 for the event.

If you are having a church wedding, make sure you ask about regulations for taking pictures in the church.

Most couples have their professional wedding photographs taken following the nuptials. This can take one to three hours. To accommodate the guests during this period of time, there can be a scheduled break of several hours between the ceremony and the reception, or you can move the guests to another area, and feed and entertain them until the pictures have been taken. We moved the guests from our backyard to our front yard, and gave them appetizers and cold glasses of lemonade while the pictures were taken and the reception tables were set up. (See suggestions of appetizers in food section)

You can also consider having the wedding photographs taken prior to the wedding.

Music and Entertainment

You can have pre-recorded music for the wedding ceremony, or pay for an organist (church), or hire a string quartet. A professional string quartet will cost about $800, however you can hire students from a university for about half that amount. You can also inquire at music schools for musicians and singers. (Make sure you audition them). If you have a talented family member or friend, you can ask them to sing or play for the ceremony and do this as a wedding gift for you.

For the reception, a Disc Jockey will cost $100-$300 per hour. You can pre-record music and ask a friend to act as a disc jockey. Again, if you have talented family members or friends, rent keyboards, microphones, and speakers (cost $200) and ask them to perform during the reception as a wedding gift. We did this at our backyard wedding and our entertainment was free. You can also hire a live band at a cost of $2000-$10,000. (If noise is going to be an issue, make sure to warn the neighbours).

Rentals

Ceremony

Chairs: I've already talked about guest chairs for an outdoor ceremony. Use the same chairs for the reception. Chairs rent for ($2-$4.25 each). You will also need a table (you may want to bring a small deck table from home) for the signing of the wedding certificate. The couple and the witnesses sign the wedding certificate directly following the ceremony.

If needed, you can rent arches and decorate them for the nuptials. White wrought iron or lattice arches rent for ($65-$150), Roman colonnade with arched top ($275-$350). You can also rent artificial trees with lights ($15-$25) if the venue is sparse.

(Tip: If the day promises to be hot, consider placing a bottle of pre-chilled water on each seat prior to the ceremony. Purchase cases of bottled water and chill in large coolers.)

Reception

Chairs: Use the chairs from the ceremony.

Tables: If you need to rent tables for the reception, plan out the space, decide on rectangular, square, or round tables, and figure out the number of tables you will need. (an 8 foot rectangular table seats 8-10 guests, a 5 foot round table seats 8-10 guests, and cost $12-$15 each).

You will also require tables for food and beverage service and a table for the wedding cake and desserts. If you are having young children at the wedding, consider having a kid's table with a brown paper tablecloth and crayons.

Tablecloths: I had several white and off-white tablecloths that we used for the food service tables, but because we chose round guest tables, I had to rent round tablecloths (white and colored, round or rectangular tablecloths cost $13-$27 each). I purchased over-sized white disposable napkins and pre-wrapped each individual set of flatware, placing the lot in a large basket beside the plates.

China, Cookware, Stemware, and Flatware: Plates and glasses are readily available in different designs and at reasonable rates (dinner or side plate $0.60-$0.85 each), (water, beer, or wine glass $0.60-$1.25 each). You can also rent serving dishes (12 quart bowls $6), (16 inch platter $6). If you are serving hot food for the reception, consider renting chafing dishes (chafing dish with fuel $20-$25 each). Flatware comes in different designs and individual utensils rent for $0.40-$0.50 each. We rented forks, knives, and dessert forks only. I supplied coffee and tea spoons. Dirty dishes and flatware are placed in bins provided by the rental company after use. (Make sure you count the flatware so that you won't be charged for lost items)

Some rental companies offer breakage insurance. Make sure you fully understand what the insurance covers before purchasing it. Four wine glasses were broken at our reception. Our insurance did not cover stains on the tablecloths. The total rental cost for our wedding was $1400, which included delivery on Friday night and pick-up on Sunday morning. (Tip: If you are planning to rent equipment for the wedding and reception book early, especially if the wedding is during wedding season as party rental places have limited stock).

Wherever the reception is being held, if you plan to have speeches you will need to rent sound equipment. Hotels, wineries, and golf clubhouses will organize the rental, but it will be at an up charge. Rent the equipment yourself from an electronics rental store and save. Assign someone to return the equipment the next day.

Portable Washrooms

Although no one likes to talk about it, toilets are an essential part of a wedding. You should have one toilet per 25-40 guests. If you have a septic field, consider renting a portable toilet. You can rent one with running water and ask the male guests to use it. Place the portable toilet in the most private place possible. (Cost $125-$150 for drop-off Friday, pick-up Monday) Assign someone to tidy up all the washrooms every half hour with fresh linens and paper. (Consider using disposable hand wipes for the guests) (Tip: If you are having a backyard wedding and do have a septic field, have it pumped out prior to the event).

Transportation

For a ceremony away from the house, bridal parties often travel in a rented limousine (Cost $50-$400 per hour with minimum hours booked). If you know someone with a luxury car, consider asking if they will drive you--they will probably be honored. Another mode of transportation is a horse drawn carriage. (Cost $200-$1000)

It is tradition to decorate the car the wedding couple will use to leave the reception. Typically plastic flowers and/or a 'just married' sign are used. (Make sure the adhesive used will not damage the car's paint)

Parking

With a backyard wedding, you need to think about parking. Let neighbours know about the date. For neighbours not invited to the ceremony, consider inviting them down for a drink and a piece of wedding cake following the guest dinner. This will hopefully prevent them from mowing their lawn during the ceremony and might deter a noise complaint. Some neighbours let us use their driveways for guest parking. We asked two male guests to arrive early and assist with parking.

Food and Beverages

Food and drink can take up a large chunk of the wedding budget. However, if you are willing to do some of the cooking and baking yourself, you can save big. A fully catered dinner affair can cost as much as $100-$200 per guest.

For a wedding with fewer guests (less than 50) consider having a barbeque. You can have salad, and purchase pre-wrapped baked potatoes (all you have to do is throw them into the oven) and serve with marinated steak, chicken, or pork.

If you are having your reception at a hotel, restaurant, or clubhouse, the way to save money is to limit the amount of food and liquor served. Instead of an open bar, only serve wine and beer, or punch only (alcohol or non-alcohol). For an open bar, think about providing 2 drink tickets per guest. The guests can purchase more tickets if they desire. For the food, consider a smorgasbord with one salad, mixed vegetables, potatoes or rice, and one meat selection. If someone absolutely can't eat the type of meat you have selected, allow them to order something from the menu. Have a simple dessert along with wedding cake, or just wedding cake. If you are having a fully served meal, usually the wedding guests are given a choice of two entrees, like chicken or fish, or chicken or beef. Again, choose reasonably priced meals and don't hesitate to ask for substitutions of sides to make the meal more cost efficient. Be prepared to pay for guests who are a no-show. Restaurants often make you guarantee the purchase of x number of meals when you book the date. (Tip: Make sure you give specific instructions to the person in charge, especially about the beverage arrangements as you don't want any surprises when you get the bill).

Chocolate fountains, candy tables and ice sculptures are fun additions, but can be expensive if catered. If you are having a backyard or hall reception and want a candy table, consider assigning someone to make it up. You can buy the candy in bulk and place it in colorful mixing bowls. Chocolate fountains including the chocolate can be rented for $175 and up.

If you are having a hall reception or backyard reception, and plan to make some or all of the food yourself like I did, read on. The total food and beverage cost for our wedding of 110 guests was just under $3,000 (about $27 per guest). For the reception, I pre-made as much of the food as I could, hiring out the making of the salads and cooking of the baron of beef. (All of the recipes I used for the wedding are in the recipe section)

For beverages, we set up a self-serve bar and served wine and beer only. Check to see if you require a liquor license in your area. We also had a selection of sodas, fruit juice and bottled water, which we placed in coolers filled with ice. We served tea and coffee after the meal. If you know you have a lot of coffee drinkers coming, think about borrowing or renting a coffee urn.

Our ceremony was at 4:00 pm and lasted 45 minutes. After the ceremony we asked the guests to move into the front yard. There they mingled and were served drinks of cold lemonade, and appetizers: bruschetta, leek tarts, and chicken and pork kabobs. (Recipes below) While the guests were in the front yard, photographs of the wedding party took place in the backyard, and assigned members of the family set up the tables for the reception. The guests were able to move back into the backyard after 30 minutes. The wedding party left to have pictures taken on a neighbour's rural property and were gone another 30 minutes.

Dinner was served at 6:30 pm. It was served in a smorgasbord style and included a green salad, curried rice salad, pasta salad, cheese plate, mashed potatoes, roasted turkey, ham, and baron of beef. There were also plates of olives, and pickles. Desserts included homemade apple pies, nanaimo bars, date squares, lemon squares, butter tarts, brownies, cookies and of course a homemade three tiered wedding cake. (Recipes below) The wedding cake was a fruit cake which I made 2 months in advance pouring liquor on weekly to preserve. The French butter icing was made and put on the cake the day of the wedding. All of the desserts with the exception of the apple pies (made by an aunt the day before the wedding) were made 4 weeks in advance. I only made squares and cookies that froze well, and had to use the freezers of two neighbours because eventually my small freezer was completely full. The kabobs were also pre-made and frozen. You can purchase frozen appetizers if time does not allow you to make them.

I hired a woman to make the salads the day before the wedding. These were recipes we tested in advance, and ones that contained no mayonnaise. This is important to prevent food poisoning especially if the day is warm. It is still recommended to put the salad bowls on trays of ice when on the table. I cooked the ham the day before the wedding and served it cold. The morning of the wedding, I put two 15 pound turkeys in the oven, both in disposable pans and covered in tinfoil. The woman I hired basted and oversaw the cooking of the turkey, as well as made the fresh tomato bruschetta and did up the potatoes. The baron of beef was purchased and cooked at a local butcher's shop, and the cost was $115. We had to assign someone to pick it up. Both the turkey and beef were served and kept warm in heated chafing pans. The cheese plates were made up the day before the wedding and placed in neighbour's fridge. Don't forget to garnish plates with parsley. I also made the leek tarts the day before the wedding. (Tip: For the quantity of food to make and portion sizes, which depends on the number of people you have attending, check on internet cooking sites).

Wedding favors are a fun part of a wedding and give the bride and groom an opportunity to visit with each guest as they hand them out. You can give something that goes with the theme of the wedding, tiny jam jars, candles, tea, chocolate, (if purchased the cost is $2-$5 per item) or you can give a favor of homemade candies or cookies. We gave three homemade heart-shaped cookies wrapped in white tulle and tied with a ribbon. (Recipe below) (Tip: You can purchase pre-cut circles of tulle in the wedding section of big box stores). We pre-made the cookies, wrapped them in tulle, and placed them in ziplock bags and put them into the freezer. On the morning of the wedding, I removed the favors and put them in a large wicker basket with a handle. On the handle of the basket I tied a wide ribbon that matched the wedding colors.

Recipes

Bruschetta (Enough made for 100 guests, but as it was a hit, there could have been more)
30 large plum tomatoes, diced
12 garlic cloves, crushed
2 cups finely chopped fresh basil
3/4 cup olive oil
3/4 cup vinegar
6 tsp salt
1 tsp pepper
6 French baguettes

Combine ingredients and let sit for 2 hours. Drain and place mixture on thinly sliced French baguettes that are toasted on one side. (Tip: we used white and whole wheat baguettes).

Leek Tarts
3/4 cup of butter
8 cups of chopped leeks
1 package of bacon, cooked and crumbled
12 eggs
6 cups whipping cream
Salt and Pepper

Make pastry or buy pre-made tart shells, prick bottoms. In a skillet, melt butter and cook leeks. Spread leeks and cooked and crumbled bacon in the pastry shells. Mix eggs, whipping cream, and seasoning and pour over the leeks and bacon. Bake at 375 degrees for 25-30 minutes until golden. Makes about 36 tarts. These should be made the day before the wedding and should not be frozen. (If you don't have enough tart pans, borrow from neighbours and friends)

Chicken and Pork Kabobs

Cut up boneless chicken and pork and let sit overnight in tenderizing sauce. The next day place on kabob sticks, put in ziplock freezer bags and place in freezer. For 100 guests, you will need to make about 50 chicken and 50 pork kabobs. On the day of the wedding the kabobs will need to be cooked until done on a barbeque. (Start cooking them just before the end of the wedding if they are to be served as appetizers before the reception).

Wild and White Rice Curried Salad (around 12 servings)

2 cups cooked white rice
1 cup cooked wild rice
1 cup celery, chopped fine
1 cup raisins, plumped up in hot water for 10 minutes and drained
1 cup red onion, chopped fine
1 cup yellow or red pepper, chopped fine
1/2 cup parsley, chopped
Salt and Pepper

Add above ingredients; then add dressing, salt and pepper to taste. Refrigerate overnight. Stir and taste in case more dressing is needed.

Dressing for Curried Salad:
4 Tbsp curry powder
1 & 1/2 cup grapeseed oil
2/3 cup Lemon Juice

Stir and chill for 2 hours to let flavors intensify. (Tip: The Wild and White Rice Curried Salad can be made the day before the wedding)

Artichoke and Pasta Salad (around 12 servings)
4 cups of cooked medium pasta
16 ounce jar of marinated artichoke hearts and liquid
2 cups cherry tomatoes, halved
2 bunches of green onions, chopped, or red onion
2 cans pitted black olives
1/2 cup chopped parsley
1 tsp dry basil
Salt and Pepper

Rinse cooked pasta with cold water several times, drain, and turn into large bowl. Mix in rest of ingredients and toss gently. Refrigerate for 4 hours or until the next day. Toss again getting liquid from the bottom of the bowl. Season with salt and pepper to taste and add more oil and lemon juice if needed.

Apple Pie (1 pie)
Crust: (I use the no fail Tenderflake lard recipe)
8 tart apples, sliced
1 cup sugar
2 Tbsp flour
2 tsp cinnamon, sprinkle 1 tsp over apples
1/2 tsp nutmeg
3 Tbsp butter

Combine sugar, flour, spices and a pinch of salt. Put sliced apples in the pastry shell, sprinkle with cinnamon and then cover with dry mixture. Dot with butter and add pastry top. Bake at 375 degrees for 50 minutes or until done.

Nanaimo Bars
3/4 cup butter
3/8 cup sugar

7 Tbsp cocoa
1 & 1/2 tsp vanilla
3 small eggs
3 cups graham wafer crumbs (30 biscuits)
2 cups coconut

Place softened butter, sugar, cocoa, vanilla and beaten eggs into a double boiler. (If you don't have a double boiler, place a smaller pot with the ingredients, into a larger pot of boiling water) Stir well until the butter has melted and the mixture resembles custard. DO NOT overcook. Remove from stove and add the crushed graham wafer crumbs and coconut. Mix and press into 9 x 13 inch greased pan and put into freezer for 15 minutes to set.

Middle layer:
3/8 cup butter
3-4 Tbsp water or milk
3 Tbsp cornstarch
3 cups of icing sugar

Cream butter, water and cornstarch, blend in icing sugar. Spread over base and return to freezer for 15 minutes.

Top layer:
6 squares of melted chocolate
2 Tbsp butter

Mix butter with melted chocolate and pour over middle layer. Let chocolate harden, then cut nanaimo bars into squares before freezing. Freeze flat in ziplock bags.

Date Squares or Matrimonial Squares
1 & 1/2 cups flour
1/2 tsp baking soda
1 tsp baking powder
1 cup butter
1 cup brown sugar
1 & 1/2 cups oatmeal

1/2 tsp salt

Filling:
1/2 lb chopped dates
1/2 cup cold water
2 Tbsp brown sugar
1/2 of an orange rind, grated
1 tsp lemon juice

Sift flour, soda, baking powder and salt. Rub in butter with finger tips. Add sugar and oatmeal and mix. Spread 1/2 of the crumbs in greased 9 x 13 baking pan and press down. Cook filling ingredients: dates, water and sugar over medium heat until thick and smooth. Remove from heat and add orange rind and lemon juice. Pour over the crumb layer and then add the rest of the oatmeal crumbs on top. Bake at 375 degrees for 30 minutes or until golden brown color. Slice into squares when cooled and freeze flat in ziplock bags.

Lemon Squares
Crust:
1 cup butter
1/2 cup icing sugar
1 cup flour
1 cup chopped nuts

Mix ingredients and press into 9 x 13 inch pan. Bake for 15 minutes at 325 degrees.

Filling:
4 eggs, beaten
1 lemon rind (can omit)
1 & 1/2 tsp baking powder
4 Tbsp flour
1/2 cup lemon juice
2 cups sugar

Mix and spread over the crust while the crust is warm. Bake

for 25 minutes at 350 degrees. Sprinkle with icing sugar when cooled. Cut into squares, put into ziplock bags, and freeze.

Butter Tarts
Make or purchase pastry shells.
Filling:
1/2 cup butter
1 & 1/2 cups brown sugar
2 eggs
2 Tbsp cream
2 tsp vanilla
1 cup raisins
1/2 cup chopped walnuts (can omit)

In a saucepan, heat butter and sugar until the butter is melted. Remove from heat and cool. Add eggs, cream, vanilla and nuts, and mix. Put some raisins in each shell and add filling mixture. (If you add the raisins to the mixture they will accumulate at the bottom of the bowl) Bake at 375 degrees for 25-30 minutes, or until golden brown.

Peppermint Brownies
1 & 1/2 cups butter
3 cups sugar
1 Tbsp vanilla
5 eggs
2 cups flour
1 cup cocoa
1 tsp baking powder
1 tsp salt
24 peppermint patties

Mix eggs, sugar and vanilla, add dry ingredients. Put one half of the batter in a greased 9 x 13 inch pan, spread the peppermint patties evenly and then add the rest of the batter. Bake at 350 degrees for 35-40 minutes or until done.

Brown Sugar Cookie Favors (300 toffee colored medium-sized cookies)
4 cups butter
7 & 1/2 cups brown sugar
8 eggs
5 tsp vanilla
12 cups flour
4 & 1/2 tsp baking soda

Mix butter and sugar, add beaten eggs, and vanilla. Add dry ingredients. Roll out dough and cut with heart-shaped cookie cutter. Put cookies on baking pan and sprinkle tops with granulated sugar. Bake at 350 degrees for 8-10 minutes. When cool, place three cookies in white tulle, and tie with ribbon. Place wrapped cookies in ziplock bags and put into freezer.

Wedding Cake

For a wedding cake you have several options. A purchased wedding cake will cost $900 and up. If you choose to bake your own cake (it is not difficult) and want a multi-tiered cake where the top layer won't sink into the bottom, it is best to bake a traditional fruit cake. The benefits of a fruit cake are that you can make it months in advance, keeping it moist by sprinkling liquor on it every few days, and can have three or four tiers because it is a very dense cake. (Recipe below) If you absolutely don't like fruit cake, the main requirement when looking for a white or chocolate cake recipe is that it is dense.

To eliminate the fuss of making three or four cakes for the tiers, you can ice and decorate Styrofoam bottoms and only have a real cake for the top tier. (It is tradition for the wedding couple to cut into the top tier and feed each other some wedding cake) If you do only have real cake for the top tier, bake and ice two or three rectangular cakes to be cut up for the guests. Another trend is to replace the wedding cake with cupcakes, placing the cupcakes on large tiered stands.

The most difficult part of the wedding cake is icing and

decorating it. I have included a French butter icing, which is delicious and easy to make. You can also take the baked cake and have it professionally decorated, about $300 and up. If you are decorating the cake, instead of using fondant roses (pre-made fondant roses can be purchased) think about edible flowers or garden roses. I decorated my daughter's cake with fresh pink roses from the garden. (Tip: wash and check fresh flowers for insects).

Wedding Fruit Cake (Triple recipe for 3 tiers, base 12 inch diameter)
2 cups butter
2 & 1/2 cups brown sugar
10 eggs
1 cup honey
1/2 cup Kahlua
4 cups flour
1 tsp baking powder
1 tsp salt
1/2 tsp cinnamon
1/2 tsp cloves
1/2 tsp mace
4 cups currants
2 cups seedless raisins
2 cups candied citron
2 cups candied pineapple
1 cup of candied cherries
1 cup candied lemon peel
1 cup candied orange peel

Mix butter and sugar and then add the rest of the ingredients, mix well. (Tip: If you don't have a large enough bowl, mix in a clean large cooler). You need to use Christmas cake tins. (If you don't know what Christmas tins are, ask a grandmother) They can be round or square, depending on what type of look you want and stack one inside another. Borrow the pans from friends or family, if possible. Pre-stack the empty pans to decide on the number of tiers. I had to purchase a larger pan for the base (cost:

$29 for a 12 inch diameter pan). Because fruit cakes take so long to bake you must line the bottoms and the sides of the pans with greased brown paper. (Tip: I double the paper and grease on both sides) Fill the pans. Put the pans on the center rack in the oven and bake at 300 degrees for 2 hours or more until cake tester comes out clean. When done, let cool and remove from pans. Place in large cooler and put cooler in cool place. Sprinkle Kahlua liquor on every five days until ready to use. (Can keep for up to 8 weeks).

Icing

You can also make an edible fondant icing, however I tried several recipes and found them all to be too chewy.

French Butter Icing
11 large egg whites
3 cups white granulated sugar
3 pounds butter (cold)
2 & 1/2 Tbsp almond flavoring

Put sugar and egg whites in a double boiler and mix continuously. Use a whisk. Heat up to 140 degrees. (Use candy thermometer) Pour into mixing bowl and beat on high until it doubles in volume. Cut up the butter into tiny bits. Add half of the butter, mix on low, then add rest of the butter mixing well. Raise the speed of the mixer and beat for 10 minutes making sure all the butter lumps have been absorbed. Add flavoring. (Tip: make up a small batch of icing to practice) This icing spreads smoothly and tastes great. Decorate cake the day of the wedding (if possible) and store in cool area.

Important Miscellaneous Items and Answers to Questions about the Wedding

Who pays: Traditionally it was the bride's parents who would pay for the wedding. Today, both sets of parents may contribute as well as the bride and groom. The parents of the groom traditionally pay for the rehearsal lunch or dinner.

Budget and Checklists: Determine your budget and then make a wedding checklist that includes approximate costs. Include the names and numbers of important contacts and note which people are responsible for what. Include plans for the honeymoon and start to think of making the travel arrangements.

Theme: Decide upon colors and a theme to enhance the day. It makes a more elegant wedding when all of the colors of the ceremony and reception are coordinated.

Marriage license: Check with the City Hall or registry in your area regarding the cost, and the number of days before the ceremony that the marriage license must be obtained. (Usually the license must be obtained 30 days before the nuptials and must be requested by the groom or bride).

Liquor License and Noise Bylaws: Check requirements in your area.

Bridal Procession and Vows: Discuss this with the person performing the ceremony. Come to the meeting with ideas of what you would like.

Beauty Appointments: Make hair, nail, and makeup appointments as soon as possible as appointments fill up, especially during wedding season.

Bridal Traditions: "Something old, something new, something borrowed, something blue" is an old saying of what things a bride should wear. Often a garter, if worn, is blue. At the reception, the throwing of the bridal bouquet or part of the bouquet is also tradition, while the groom would remove and throw the garter.

Speeches: Traditionally at the reception speeches are given by the best man, maid of honor, and father of the bride. The groom may also give a speech. During the rehearsal luncheon or dinner, the groom's father may give a speech.

Guestbook: Assign a young person to get guest signatures upon arrival.

Decorations and Centerpieces: Use the wedding colors and be creative with the centerpieces incorporating the theme of the wedding. Look at wedding pictures on the internet to get ideas. Consider seating cards if you want guests to sit at certain tables.

Lighting: Consider putting white Christmas lights in the trees, solar lights in the garden and tea lights on the tables.

Kitchen Help and Servers: If you are doing the food yourself, you will need to hire one or two people to help out in the kitchen. Just make sure they can cook! We hired the grandmother of one of the bridesmaids. You will also require one server per 20-25 guests. We asked the daughters of some neighbours and friends. (Cost per hour $15-$20). They should serve appetizers, set up food table, clear tables, and scrape and stack the plates for rental pickup.

Security: Unfortunately there are thefts of wedding gifts and cards that might contain gifts of money. Assign the groomsmen to collect the presents and cards when the guests arrive and place them in a locked or secure area.

When do the bride and groom leave the reception? There is no set rule. However, don't forget to make a reservation at a hotel, if you plan to spend the wedding night in town.

Other things to think about: You will need to purchase gifts to give to the wedding party attendants. The gifts are given at the rehearsal luncheon or dinner. You will also need to buy wedding bands. Purchase or make a Ring bearer's pillow, if required.

Cleanup and Garbage: If you are putting on the reception be prepared for a large amount of garbage. We filled 3 large cans with garbage and had 7 bags of paper recycling (the recycling included wrapping paper from the gifts). The cleanup will go more swiftly if you have help. Ask family members to volunteer. It took three of us three hours to clean the tables and area, and to pull apart and stack the tables and chairs.

Thank You Cards: It is proper etiquette to send a thank you card within a year of the wedding. Consider including a photograph of the big day.

Wedding Brunch the following day: Traditionally the bride's family holds a brunch the following day, where the bride and groom and their families gather to open presents. Don't forget to have someone document the gift and the name of the giver. For the meal, incorporate the leftovers from the wedding reception. If you had a catered reception, plan a simple meal (fruit, vegetables, sliced meats, cheese, buns and muffins) for the brunch. You may want to serve a light punch, champagne and orange juice, or just tea and coffee. And then relax and enjoy the gathering.

Note: As the cost of a wedding solely depends on the location, please be aware that some items may cost more or less than quoted. It is very important to determine what you want, and to check out the costs in your area, so that you will not overspend your predetermined budget.

ABOUT THE AUTHOR

D.P. Scott has had years of experience in planning and organizing large group events on a budget. This guidebook is a result of her using this knowledge to save thousands of dollars on her daughter's formal wedding. Other titles by D.P. Scott can be found at www.dpscott.ca.

www.ingramcontent.com/pod-product-compliance
Lightning Source LLC
Chambersburg PA
CBHW060705280326
41933CB00012B/2315